# Springs of Devotion

Inspiring Writings
About the Meaning
and Joy of Prayer

Selected by
Arthur Wortman
Illustrated by
William Gilmore

HALLMARK EDITIONS

# Contents

# The Gift of Prayer

---

## 'I AM THE WAY'

We think we must climb to a certain height of goodness before we can reach God. But He says not, "At the end of the end of the end of the way you may find me"; He says "I am the Way; I am the road under your feet, the road that begins just as low down as you happen to be." If we are in a hole the Way begins in a hole. The moment we set our face in the same direction as His, we are walking with God.

HELEN WODEHOUSE

## A FERVENT SPIRIT

He who prays must address God as though he were in His presence; inasmuch as the Lord is everywhere, in every place, in every man, and especially in the soul of the just. Therefore let us not seek God on earth, nor in heaven, nor elsewhere; rather let us seek Him in our own heart, like unto the prophet that sayeth, "I will hearken unto that which the Lord shall say in me."

In prayer a man may take heed to his words, and this is a wholly material thing; he may take heed to the sense of his words, and this is rather study than prayer; finally, he may fix his thoughts on God, and this is the only true prayer. We must consider neither the words nor the sentences, but lift our soul above our self, and almost lose self in the thought of God. This state once attained, the believer forgets the world and worldly desires, and has, as it were, a foreshadowing of heavenly bliss.

To this height it is as easy for the ignorant as for the learned to rise. Words, in fact, are not essential to prayer; on the contrary, when man is truly rapt in the spirit of devotion, speech is an impediment, and should be replaced by mental prayer. Thus it is seen how great is the error of those that prescribe a fixed number of orations. The Lord taketh joy not in a multitude of words, but rather in a fervent spirit.

GIROLAMO SAVONAROLA

Prayer is and remains always the native and deepest impulse of the soul of man.

THOMAS CARLYLE

## PRAYER OUR ANSWER

To pray is to take notice of the wonder, to regain a sense of the mystery that animates all beings, the divine margin in all attainments. Prayer is *our* humble *answer* to the inconceivable surprise of living.                                    ABRAHAM J. HESCHEL

## GOD'S HELP

"Get the distaff ready, and God will send the flax."                                    —My Grandmother
These were words my grandmother used to say. She said them, not as a promise or an admonition, but as a simple statement of fact about the way the world worked. I used to spend a lot of time thinking what it meant. The distaff was a man-made tool, shaped for a special purpose, that of making thread. It was intended for no other use. So the proverb, I decided, meant that we must "meet God halfway," doing our best to help ourselves. But also, it meant we have to be specifically ready for opportunity, not just virtuously sitting around waiting for a call from heaven. We have to know exactly what we mean to do, and be fully prepared to do it—with God's help.                                    MARGARET MEAD

## TO BE ALONE WITH GOD

If we are not to lose ourselves in that real loneliness which is remoteness from God, we must have periods of loneliness upon earth when our soul is left to itself and we are remote from other men. It is an historical achievement of Israel that through prayer it satisfied this human need and religious necessity. The purpose of prayer is to allow us to be alone with God and apart from other men, to give us seclusion in the midst of the world.                    LEO BAECK

## POWER TO COMPREHEND

Just as the anatomist, given the fragment of a human skull, can reconstruct with reasonable certainty many other characteristics of the head and even the rest of the human body, so the religious mind, repeatedly plumbing the depths of human experience, may have a faint twilight perception of the constitution of the universe itself; though no finite mind will ever grasp it fully or exhaust all its possibilities until the end of time: for time, in all its organic and human implications, is part of what must be revealed.

LEWIS MUMFORD

# PRAYER

*is our humble answer to the inconceivable surprise of living.*

---

ABRAHAM J. HESCHEL

He who gives up regularity in prayer has lost a principal means of reminding himself that spiritual life is obedience to a Lawgiver, not a mere feeling or taste.  CARDINAL NEWMAN

Prayer is the soul's sincere desire,
    Uttered or unexpressed,
The motion of a hidden fire
    That trembles in the breast.
Prayer is the burden of a sigh,
    The falling of a tear,
The upward glancing of an eye
    When none but God is near.

JAMES MONTGOMERY

## PRAYER COVERS EVERYTHING

Prayer covers the whole of a man's life. There is no thought, feeling, yearning, or desire, however low, trifling or vulgar we may deem it, which, if it affects our real interest and happiness, we may not lay before God and be sure of sympathy. His nature is such that our often coming does not tire him. The whole burden of the whole life of every man may be rolled on to God and not weary him, though it has wearied the man.  HENRY WARD BEECHER

# PHILOSOPHY AND PRAYER

God is both in us and out of us; He is both immanent and transcendent. There can be no fundamental contradiction between God as known to philosophic thought and God as known to personal devotion. In philosophy we seek to know God and to honor him through our intelligence; in devotion we approach Him through love and adoration. We have ample warrant for confidence that neither quest is in vain.

WILLIAM R. INGE

Thou hast made us for Thyself, and our heart is restless until it finds repose in Thee.

ST. AUGUSTINE

Prayer is not asking for things—not even for the best things. It is going where they are.

GEORGE HEARD

It is God Himself who prays through us, when we pray to Him. . . . We cannot bridge the gap between God and ourselves through even the most intensive and frequent prayers; the gap between God and ourselves can only be bridged by God.

PAUL TILLICH

I have sought
thy nearness,
With all my heart
I called thee,
And going out
to meet thee,
I found thee
coming toward
me.

As down in the sunless retreats of the ocean,
Sweet flowers are springing no mortals can see,
So, deep in my soul the still prayer of devotion
Unheard by the world rises silent to thee.

THOMAS MOORE

## OUR KNOWLEDGE OF GOD

In the case of our human friends we take their existence for granted, not caring whether it is proven or not. Our relationship is such that we could read philosophical arguments designed to prove the non-existence of each other, and perhaps even be convinced by them—and then laugh together over so odd a conclusion.

I think that it is something of the same kind of security we should seek in our relationship with God. The most flawless proof of the existence of God is no substitute for it; and if we have that relationship the most convincing disproof is turned harmlessly aside. If I may say it with reverence, the soul and God laugh together over so odd a conclusion.

SIR ARTHUR EDDINGTON

We can prove the reality of prayer only by praying. SHERWOOD EDDY

*Prayer is
and remains always
the native and deepest
impulse of the soul
of man.*

———

THOMAS CARLYLE

into it, entering by it into communion with Him of whom it is a part; recognizing oneself as the slave of God; and testing oneself, one's actions, one's desires, according to the demands not of the external circumstances of the world but of this divine part of one's soul.     LEO TOLSTOY

## MY TASK IS SIMPLE

As I analyze myself I find several things happening to me as a result of these two months of strenuous effort to keep God in mind every minute. This concentration upon God is strenuous, but everything else has ceased to be so. I think more clearly, I forget less frequently. Things which I did with a strain before, I now do easily and with no effort whatever. I worry about nothing, and lose no sleep. I walk on air a good part of the time. Even the mirror reveals a new light in my eyes and face. I no longer feel in a hurry about anything. Everything goes right. Each minute I meet calmly as though it were not important. Nothing can go wrong excepting one thing. . . . God *may slip from my mind* if I do not keep on my guard. If He is there, the universe is with me.

My task is simple and clear.  FRANK LAUBACH

## CHRIST'S INSTRUCTIONS
## FOR PRAYER

And when thou prayest, thou shalt not be as the hypocrites are: for they love to pray standing in the synagogues and in the corners of the streets, that they may be seen of men. Verily I say unto you, They have their reward.

But thou, when thou prayest, enter into thy closet, and when thou hast shut thy door, pray to thy Father which is in secret; and thy Father which seeth in secret shall reward thee openly.

But when ye pray, use not vain repetitions, as the heathen do: for they think that they shall be heard for their much speaking.

Be not ye therefore like unto them: for your Father knoweth what things ye have need of, before ye ask him.                    MATTHEW 6:5-8

## GOD IS EVERYWHERE

Begin prayer by recalling the presence of God. You will soon feel the benefit of such a practice. God is everywhere. There is no place where he is not. Let birds fly where they will, they always encounter air; so we are always where God is.

ST. FRANCOIS DE SALES

## BELIEVE WHEN YOU PRAY

Whosoever shall say unto this mountain, Be thou removed and be thou cast into the sea; and shall not doubt in his heart, but shall believe that those things which he saith shall come to pass; he shall have whatsoever he saith. Therefore I say unto you, What things soever ye desire, when ye pray, believe that ye receive them, and ye shall receive them.        MARK 11:23-24

## GOD HEARS ALL

Numberless as the sands are those who have life and being through Thee. And yet, Thou hearest the cry of all the creatures, and the cry of man whom Thou hast specially formed. Thou hearest the cry of all men without confusing their mixed voices and without distinguishing one from another in such a way as to play favorites.

Thou hearest not only the voice of one who is responsible for many others and so prays to Thee in their name, as if his high function could bring him nearer to Thee: Thou hearest not only the voice of one who prays for dear ones, as if he could thereby attract Thine attention, he who is privileged in having the dear ones; no Thou hearest also the most miserable, the most abandoned, the most solitary man—in the desert, in the multitude. Thou hast not forgotten him. Thou rememberest his name. . . .

And if in the thick shadows of dread, in the prey of terrible thoughts, he was abandoned by men, abandoned almost by the language men speak, still Thou wouldst not have forgotten him. Thou wouldst understand his language.

SOREN KIERKEGAARD

The Great Rabbi of Porischa became dangerously ill, and the inhabitants of his town proclaimed a fast for his speedy convalescence. A man chanced to come to town and went to the tavern for a drink of brandy. Several townsfolk overheard him and informed him that drinking was prohibited for the day.

The man went at once to the synagogue and prayed: "O Lord, please cure the Holy Rabbi so that I may have a drink."

Soon thereafter the Rabbi began to recover his strength, and he then declared to his followers: "The prayer of that man was more acceptable than any of yours. He expressed the greatest longing, and the most earnest supplication, for my recovery." HASIDIC TALE

HE *that planted the ear, shall He not hear?*

HE *that formed the eye, shall He not see?*

PSALMS 94:9

## PRAYER AND LOVE

True prayer is only another name for the love of God. Its excellence does not consist in the multitude of our words; for our Father knoweth what things we have need of before we ask Him. The true prayer is that of the heart, and the heart prays only for what it desires. To pray, then, is to desire—but to desire what God would have us desire. He who desires not from the bottom of his heart, offers a deceitful prayer.

FRANCOIS FENELON

The daily prayers of the faithful make satisfaction for those daily, tiny faults from which this life cannot be free.          ST. AUGUSTINE

## PITFALLS OF PRAYER

There are two main pitfalls on the road to mastery of the art of prayer. If a person gets what he asks for, his humility is in danger. If he fails to get what he asks for, he is apt to lose confidence. Indeed, no matter whether prayer seems to be succeeding or failing, humility and confidence are two virtues which are absolutely essential.          A TRAPPIST MONK

Live among men as if God beheld you; speak with God as if men were listening.　SENECA

When thou prayest, rather let thy heart be without words than thy words without heart.

ANONYMOUS

## INTERCESSION IN PRAYER

What is Prayer? In a most general sense, it is the intercourse of our little human souls with God. Therefore it includes all the work done by God Himself through, in, and with the souls which are self-given to him in prayer. . . .

The saints show us that real intercession is not merely a petition but a piece of work, involving perfect, costly self-surrender to God for the work He wants done on other souls. Such great self-giving and great results may be their special privilege; still, they are showing us on a grand scale something which each cell of the Body of Christ has got to try to do on a small scale. They prove to us how closely and really all human spirits are connected—what we can do for one another if we only love enough—and how far-reaching is the power and responsibility of every Christian soul. We can only understand

23

their experience by realizing that we are truly parts of a great spiritual organism. The Mystical Body of Christ is not an image, but a fact. We perpetually give and take from each other the indwelling Divine Life, and by our prayers, thoughts and actions affect all within our radius.

EVELYN UNDERHILL

## THE PRAYER OF FAITH

Is any one among you suffering? Let him pray. Is any cheerful? Let him sing praise. Is any among you sick? Let him call for the elders of the church, and let them pray over him, anointing him with oil in the name of the Lord; and the prayer of faith will save the sick man, and the Lord will raise him up; and if he has committed sins, he will be forgiven. Therefore confess your sins to one another, and pray for one another, that you may be healed.

The prayer of a righteous man has great power in its effects. Elijah was a man of like nature with ourselves and he prayed fervently that it might not rain, and for three years and six months it did not rain on the earth. Then he prayed again and the heaven gave rain, and the earth brought forth its fruit.     JAMES 5:13-18

WE MUST LEARN
*that to expect God
to do everything
while we do
nothing
is not faith,
but superstition.*

———————

MARTIN LUTHER KING, JR.

Those who pray as Christ taught us to pray are never praying against each other; for they do not pray that their own will may be done, but God's.                    WILLIAM TEMPLE

## MANY FORMS OF PRAYER

I came to realize that many prayers are uttered without the prescribed forms of piety and even in a language which Puritans might, in their rigidity and lovelessness, label as profane. . . . If you will listen, you can hear prayers in the novels, songs, plays, and films of Samuel Beckett, Ralph Ellison, Ingmar Bergman, Saul Bellow, Bob Dylan, Tennessee Williams, James Baldwin, William Golding, Michelangelo Antonioni, Jean Genet, or John Updike. Prayer bridges the heretical gulf between the sacred and the secular, the holy and profane. Of course, to hear some prayers, verbal or nonverbal, you must *listen* for what was not said. . . .

Each of us is a person, with individual masks, scars, celebrations, moments of rejecting God, and experiences of conversion. Our prayers must spring from the indigenous soil of our own personal confrontation with the Spirit of God in our lives.                    MALCOLM BOYD

# I KNOW THAT GOD HEARS PRAYER

I know that God hears prayer.
Although the burdens may
Seem greater than the heart can bear,
Still, day by day,
He eases them: a little here, a little there,
In answer, and some fitting hour
Along the road,
He stoops and lifts the load,
And bids us go, lighthearted, glad,
Stronger through testings we have had.

I know that God hears prayer.
We lift our praise,
And through his bright eternal days
The sound comes clear—
Like music to his ear.
Yea, every word of every prayer
Loosed on the air
Will bring an answer if we wait,
Though it come soon or late.

GRACE NOLL CROWELL

*Thou hast
made us
for Thyself,
and our heart
is restless
until it finds
repose in Thee.*

———

ST. AUGUSTINE

# PRAYER AND WORK

The idea that man expects God to do everything leads inevitably to a callous misuse of prayer. For if God does everything, man then asks him for anything, and God becomes little more than a "cosmic bellhop" who is summoned for every trivial need. Or God is considered so omnipotent and man so powerless that prayer is a substitute for work and intelligence. . . .

God, who gave us minds for thinking and bodies for working, would defeat his own purpose if he permitted us to obtain through prayer what may come through work and intelligence. Prayer is a marvelous and necessary supplement of our feeble efforts, but it is a dangerous substitute.

When Moses strove to lead the Israelites to the Promised Land, God made it clear that he would not do for them what they could do for themselves. "And the Lord said unto Moses, Wherefore criest thou unto me? Speak unto the children of Israel, that they go forward. . . ."

We must never feel that God will, through some breathtaking miracle or a wave of the hand, cast evil out of the world. As long as we believe this we will pray unanswerable prayers

mind is swimming with clear concepts and bril-
liant purposes and easy acts of love. . . .

It is the will to pray that is the essence of
prayer, and the desire to find God, to see Him
and to love Him is the one thing that matters. If
you have desired to know Him and love Him,
you have already done what was expected of
you. . . .

No matter how distracted you may be, pray
by peaceful, even perhaps inarticulate, efforts to
center your heart upon God, Who is present in
you in spite of all that may be going through
your mind. His presence does not depend on
your thoughts of Him. He is unfailingly there;
if He were not, you could not even exist. The
memory of His unfailing presence is the surest
anchor for our minds and hearts in the storm of
distraction and temptation by which we must be
purified.                          THOMAS MERTON

Grant us grace, Almighty Father, so to pray as
to deserve to be heard.            JANE AUSTEN

Only a theoretical deity is left to any man who
has ceased to commune with God, and a theoretical deity saves no man from sin and disheart-
enment.            HARRY EMERSON FOSDICK

# TELL HIM

The little sharp vexations
    And the briars that cut the feet,
Why not take all to the Helper
    Who has never failed us yet?
Tell Him about the heartache,
    And tell Him the longings too,
Tell Him the baffled purpose
    When we scarce know what to do.
Then, leaving all our weakness
    With the One divinely strong,
Forget that we bore the burden
    And carry away the song.

PHILLIPS BROOKS

## WHEN GOD SPEAKS TO US

It is true that the voice of God, when we hear it, speaks in the very cadence of our own voice, the very idiom of our own mind. But I don't regard that as cause for suspicion. I can't see why God shouldn't be perfectly at home in the subconscious.

His remarks to me tend to be pretty short and snappy. They usually depress my pretensions, as Jane Austen might have put it; they often make me laugh; and they always—this, really, is why I believe they're authentic messages— they always cheer me up and stiffen my spine. Temporarily, because of my sins, but every little bit helps.

Or sometimes it's a saint conveying the message. For instance: Walking out of my room one difficult, disorganized day, on my way downstairs to a confusion of duties I didn't feel up to coping with, my eye lit on St. Thérèse.

"Help!" I exclaimed, without ceremony. And she: "Go without."

I was really taken aback. And yet it was so like her—so exactly what she would say. I went on downstairs laughing, and got through it all somehow. So, she answered, and refused, and the refusal was all the help I needed. Just the sort of paradox Heaven seems to delight in.

FAE MALANIA


He that planted the ear, shall He not hear?
He that formed the eye, shall He not see?

PSALMS 94:9


A good prayer, though often used, is still fresh and fair in the ears and eyes of Heaven.

THOMAS FULLER

I have been driven many times upon my knees by the overwhelming conviction that I had nowhere else to go. My own wisdom and that of all about me seemed insufficient for that day.

ABRAHAM LINCOLN

## THE PRACTICE OF THE PRESENCE OF GOD

1.   The most holy, common and necessary practice in the spiritual life is *the practice of the presence of God*; that is, habitually to take pleasure in His divine company, speaking humbly and conversing with Him lovingly at all seasons, at every minute, without rule or measure—above all, in the time of temptations, sorrows, dryness, distaste, even of infidelities and sins.

2.   One must try continually so that all his actions without distinction may be a sort of little conversation with God; however, not in a studied way, but just as they happen, with purity and simplicity of heart.

3.   We must do all our actions with deliberation and care, without impetuosity or precipitation, for these show a disordered spirit. We must work gently, calmly and lovingly with God, and beg Him to accept our work. . . .

4. During our work and other actions, even during our reading and writing on spiritual topics, more—during our exterior devotions and vocal prayers—let us stop a few minutes, as often as we can, to adore God in the depths of our hearts, to enjoy Him, as it were, in passing and in secret. Since you are not unaware that God is present before you during your actions, that He is in the depth and center of your heart, why should you not cease your exterior occupations—at least, from time to time—and even your vocal prayers, to adore Him interiorly, to praise, petition Him, to offer Him your heart, and to thank Him?

What can there be more pleasing to God than thus a thousand times a day to leave all creatures in order to retire and worship Him in one's interior. . . .

5. All this adoration should be made by faith, believing that God really is in our hearts; that he is truth; that He sees all that passes and will pass within us and in all creatures; that He is independent of all, the One upon Whom all creatures depend. In justice we owe Him all our thoughts, words and actions.

6. We must carefully examine which are the virtues most necessary for us, those most diffi-

*Lord, make me*
*an instrument*
*of your* PEACE.
*Where there is*
*hatred, let me sow*
LOVE.

ST. FRANCIS OF ASSISI

cult to acquire, the sins into which we most frequently fall, and the most usual and unavoidable occasions of our falls. In the time of struggle we should have recourse to God with entire confidence and remain in the presence of His divine Majesty. We ought to adore Him humbly, declare to Him our misery and weakness, lovingly beg the aid of His grace. By this means shall we find in Him all virtues, even though we do not possess one.                BROTHER LAWRENCE

A single grateful thought toward Heaven is the most perfect prayer.                G. E. LESSING

It is not well for a man to pray cream, and live skim milk.                HENRY WARD BEECHER

## A TWO-FOLD WORSHIP

The words "to worship" mean to stoop and bow down the body with external gestures; to serve in the work. But to worship God in spirit is the service and honor of the heart; it comprehends faith and fear in God. The worshipping of God is two-fold, outward and inward—that is, to acknowledge God's benefits, and to be thankful unto Him.                MARTIN LUTHER

# PRAYER IN AN
## UNPREDICTABLE WORLD

[It is said that] if man's freedom is to be of any value, if he is to have any power of planning and of adapting means to ends, he must live in a predictable world. But if God alters the course of events in answer to prayer, then the world will be unpredictable. Therefore, if man is to be effectively free, God must be in this respect unfree.

But is it not plain that this predictable world, whether it is necessary to our freedom or no, is not the world we live in? This is a world of bets and insurance policies, of hopes and anxieties, where "nothing is certain but the unexpected" and prudence lies in "the masterly administration of the unforeseen." Nearly all the things people pray about are unpredictable: the result of a battle or an operation, the losing or getting of a job, the reciprocation of a love. We don't pray about eclipses.                C. S. LEWIS

To pray together, in whatever tongue or ritual, is the most tender brotherhood of hope and sympathy that men can contract in this life.

MADAME DE STAEL

## WHEN THE SPIRIT IS DRY

What shall we do about the "dry times," about the seasons when all the desire for prayer has left us and when prayer is the last thing in which we feel we want to engage? Isn't it wrong to force ourselves to pray?...

All prayer reaches plateaus where it loses the initial exhilaration of climbing. These are the times when a consolidation of our commitment may be taking place. In such times the testing of our real loyalty is in process. Anyone can pray when the heart is bubbling over; no loyalty is needed then. But when the spirit is dry and all surface desire gone, then is the time when we learn to whom we really belong. No one has expressed this better than François de Sales, who insists that when we cannot give God fresh roses, we give him dry ones, for "the dry have more strength and sweetness."

DOUGLAS V. STEERE

We, ignorant of ourselves,
Beg often our own harms, which the wise powers
Deny us for our good; so find we profit
By losing of our prayers.

WILLIAM SHAKESPEARE

*Our* FATHER
*which art in heaven,*
*Hallowed* MATTHEW
6:9-13
*be thy name.*

# A Little Treasury of Great Prayers

---

## MY PRAYER

Great God, I ask Thee for no meaner pelf
Than that I may not disappoint myself;
That in my action I may soar as high
As I can now discern with this clear eye.

And next in value, which thy kindness lends,
That I may greatly disappoint my friends,
Howe'er they think or hope that it may be
They may not dream how thou'st
   distinguished me.

That my weak hand may equal my firm faith,
And my life practise more than my tongue saith;
   That my low conduct may not show,
     Nor my relenting lines,
   That I thy purpose did not know,
     Or overrated thy designs.

HENRY DAVID THOREAU

## FROM *THE ROCK*

O Light Invisible, we praise Thee!
Too bright for mortal vision.
O Greater Light, we praise Thee for the less;
The eastern light our spires touch at morning,
The light that slants upon our western doors
    at evening,
The twilight over stagnant pools at batflight,
Moon light and star light, owl and moth light,
Glow-worm glowlight on a grassblade.

O Light Invisible, we worship Thee!
    We thank Thee for the lights
      that we have kindled,
The light of altar and of sanctuary;
Small lights of those who meditate at midnight
And lights directed through
    the coloured panes of windows
And light reflected from the polished stone,
The gilded carven wood, the coloured fresco.
Our gaze is submarine, our eyes look upward
And see the light that fractures through
    unquiet water.
We see the light but see not whence it comes.
O Light Invisible, we glorify Thee!

T. S. ELIOT

43

*I* will lift up
mine eyes
unto the hills,
from whence
cometh PSALM 121
   my help.

They say that everyone has his own cross to bear, Lord. And you once said, "Take up your cross and follow me." What do these things mean? I think they mean that every person ultimately has to face up to reality—face his own destiny, his own calling, his own nature and responsibilities.

In your own life, Jesus, you faced reality directly and unequivocally. You incarnated the truth as you believed it. You didn't pander to any easy or obvious popularity. You attacked the hypocrisies of the human power structure head on. You rejected the status quo in favor of obedience to the Kingdom of God. And when it came to taking the consequences, you didn't shy away from the most difficult forms of torture and execution.

The way of the cross was your understanding of your mission and your faithfulness to it.

The way of the cross seems to be, for every individual Christian, the reality which dictates his style of life, defines his own mission, and brings him into communion with you.

Help me bear my cross on the way of the cross, Jesus.　　　MALCOLM BOYD

45

## THESE THREE THINGS

O God, give us the serenity to accept
What cannot be changed;
Courage to change what should be changed,
And wisdom to distinguish one from the other.

REINHOLD NIEBUHR

## I WILL LIFT UP MINE EYES

I will lift up mine eyes unto the hills, from whence cometh my help.

My help cometh from the Lord, which made heaven and earth.

He will not suffer thy foot to be moved: he that keepeth thee will not slumber.

Behold, he that keepeth Israel shall neither slumber nor sleep.

The Lord is thy keeper: the Lord is thy shade upon thy right hand.

The sun shall not smite thee by day, nor the moon by night.

The Lord shall preserve thee from all evil: he shall preserve thy soul.

The Lord shall preserve thy going out and thy coming in from this time forth, and even for evermore.                    PSALM 121

# TO WALK THE NARROW WAY

Give me Thy grace, good Lord,
To set the world at nought,
To set my mind fast upon Thee.
And not to hang upon the blast of men's mouths.
To be content to be solitary,
Not to long for worldly company,
Little and little utterly to cast off the world,
And rid my mind of all the business thereof.
Not to long to hear of any worldly things,
But that the hearing of worldly phantasies
    may be to me displeasant.
Gladly to be thinking of God,
Piteously to call for His help,
To lean unto the comfort of God,
Busily to labour to love Him.
To know mine own vility and wretchedness,
To humble and meeken myself
    under the mighty hand of God,
To bewail my sins passed,
For the purging of them,
    patiently to suffer adversity.
Gladly to bear my purgatory here,
To be joyful of tribulations,
To walk the narrow way that leadeth to life.

ST. THOMAS MORE

## THE LORD BLESS THEE

The Lord bless thee, and keep thee;
The Lord make His face to shine upon thee,
   and be gracious unto thee;
The Lord lift up His countenance upon thee,
   and give thee peace.

NUMBERS 6:24-26

## TO THE SUPREME BEING

The prayers I make will then be sweet indeed
If Thou the spirit give by which I pray:
My unassisted heart is barren clay,
That of its native self can nothing feed:
Of good and pious works thou art the seed,
That quickens only where thou say'st it may:
Unless Thou show to us thine own true way
No man can find it: Father! Thou must lead.
Do Thou, then, breathe those thoughts
   into my mind
By which such virtue may in me be bred
That in thy holy footsteps I may tread;
The fetters of my tongue do Thou unbind,
That I may have the power to sing of thee,
And sound thy praises everlastingly.

MICHELANGELO BUONARROTI

# IN THANKFUL REMEMBRANCE FOR MY DEAR HUSBAND'S SAFE ARRIVAL, SEPTEMBER 3, 1662

What shall I render to thy name,
Or how thy praises speak;
My thanks how shall I testify?
O Lord, thou knowest I'm weak.

What did I ask for but thou gavest?
What could I more desire?
But thankfulness, even all my days,
I humbly this require.

Thy mercies, Lord, have been so great,
In number numberless,
Impossible for to recount
Or any way express.

ANNE BRADSTREET

## IN THE GARDEN OF THE LORD

Teach it again to us, O living God! Teach us to renew ourselves, O Jesus, Who wept bitter tears in Gethsemane.

Help us to forget the long way of pain and strife we have come, each of us dragging a cross to some Calvary in our hearts. Help us to forget the hours of utter darkness when we have lost the way. Help us to forget our hates, fears and the bitter thoughts that divide us.

Help us to remember the upclimbing will that is a staff unto our feet. Nourish in us every tiny impulse to help each other. Give us more love, more compassion, more sincerity one to another.

Help us to appreciate the present moment and to search out its advantages that we may be glad for the todays of life, leaving the tomorrows in Thy Hand.

Steady us to do our full stint of work. Help us to rise each day with new sympathies, new thoughts of unity and joy.    HELEN KELLER

## SOCRATES' PRAYER

Beloved Pan, and all ye other gods who haunt this place! Give me beauty in the inward soul; and may the outward and inward man be as one. May I reckon the wise to be the wealthy, and may I have such a quantity of gold as a temperate man, and he only, can bear and carry.—Anything more? This prayer, I think, is enough for me.

FROM THE *PHAEDRUS*

O God, give us
the SERENITY
to accept
What cannot
be changed;
COURAGE
to change
what should be
changed,
And WISDOM
to distinguish
one from
the other.

REINHOLD NIEBUHR

Give me
Thy grace,
good LORD,
To set the world
at nought,
To set my mind
fast upon Thee.

ST. THOMAS MORE

## THE LORD IS MY SHEPHERD

The Lord is my shepherd; I shall not want.

He maketh me to lie down in green pastures: he leadeth me beside the still waters.

He restoreth my soul: he leadeth me in the paths of righteousness for his name's sake.

Yea, though I walk through the valley of the shadow of death, I will fear no evil: for thou art with me; thy rod and thy staff they comfort me.

Thou preparest a table before me in the presence of mine enemies: thou anointest my head with oil; my cup runneth over.

Surely goodness and mercy shall follow me all the days of my life: and I will dwell in the house of the Lord for ever.           PSALM 23

## THOU HAST LOVED US FIRST

Father in Heaven! Thou has loved us first, help us never to forget that Thou art love so that this sure conviction might triumph in our hearts over the seduction of the world, over the inquietude of the soul, over the anxiety for the future, over the fright of the past, over the distress of the moment. But grant also that this conviction might discipline our soul so that our heart might remain faithful and sincere in the love which we bear to all those whom Thou hast commanded us to love as we love ourselves.

SOREN KIERKEGAARD

## O LORD, MY STRENGTH

Let the words of my mouth, and the meditation of my heart, be acceptable in thy sight, O Lord, my strength, and my redeemer. PSALMS 19:14

## THE PATIENCE OF GOD

God of our fathers and our God, give us the faith to believe in the ultimate triumph of righteousness, no matter how dark and uncertain are the skies of today.

We pray for the bifocals of faith—that see the despair and the need of the hour but also see, further on, the patience of our God working out His plan in the world He has made.

Make our faith honest by helping us this day to do one thing because Thou hast said, "Do it," or to abstain because Thou hast said, "Thou shalt not."

May our faith be seen in our works. Amen.

PETER MARSHALL

# A HYMN

*After reading "Lead, Kindly Light"*

Lead gently, Lord, and slow,
　　For oh, my steps are weak,
And ever as I go,
　　Some soothing sentence speak;

That I may turn my face
　　Through doubt's obscurity
Toward thine abiding-place,
　　E'en tho' I cannot see.

For lo, the way is dark;
　　Through mist and cloud I grope,
Save for that fitful spark,
　　The little flame of hope.

Lead gently, Lord, and slow,
　　For fear that I may fall;
I know not where to go
　　Unless I hear thy call.

My fainting soul doth yearn
　　For thy green hills afar;
So let thy mercy burn—
　　My greater, guiding star!

PAUL LAURENCE DUNBAR

# LORD, WHERE SHALL I FIND THEE?

Lord, where shall I find thee?
High and hidden is thy place;
And where shall I not find thee?
The world is full of thy glory.

I have sought thy nearness,
With all my heart I called thee,
And going out to meet thee
I found thee coming toward me.

JUDAH HALEVI

## AFTER ST. AUGUSTINE

Sunshine let it be or frost,
    Storm or calm, as Thou shalt choose;
Though Thine every gift were lost,
    Thee thyself we could not lose.

MARY ELIZABETH COLERIDGE

## THESE ARE THE GIFTS I ASK

These are the gifts I ask
Of thee, Spirit serene:
Strength for the daily task,
Courage to face the road,

Good cheer to help me bear the traveller's load,
And, for the hours of rest that come between,
An inward joy in all things heard and seen.
These are the sins I fain
Would have thee take away:
Malice, and cold disdain,
Hot anger, sullen hate,
Scorn of the lowly, envy of the great,
And discontent that casts a shadow gray
On all the brightness of a common day.

HENRY VAN DYKE


## THE LORD'S PRAYER

Our Father which art in heaven, Hallowed be thy name.

Thy kingdom come, Thy will be done in earth, as it is in heaven.

Give us this day our daily bread.

And forgive us our debts, as we forgive our debtors.

And lead us not into temptation, but deliver us from evil: For thine is the kingdom, and the power, and the glory, for ever. Amen.

MATTHEW 6:9-13